Original title:
Balancing Bonds

Author: Linda Leevike
ISBN HARDBACK: 978-9916-86-968-0
ISBN PAPERBACK: 978-9916-86-969-7
ISBN EBOOK: 978-9916-86-970-3

In the Midst of Connection

In the quiet hum of night,
Whispers dance between the stars,
Hearts entwined in soft delight,
Beneath the moon's gentle bars.

Through the shadows, voices call,
Echoes of a shared embrace,
In this moment, we stand tall,
Time suspended in our space.

Words like threads, they weave a bond,
Connecting souls, deep and wide,
In the silence, we respond,
Finding comfort side by side.

Distance melts, like morning frost,
Each heartbeat a path to trace,
In this journey, love embossed,
Finding solace in each face.

In the midst of joy and pain,
We rise and fall, a rhythmic song,
Through the storms and gentle rain,
Together is where we belong.

Light and Shadow of Affection

In the dawn, warmth glows bright,
Promises whisper in soft light.
Yet shadows stretch with the day,
In love's dance, we find our way.

Under stars, secrets unfold,
Every touch, a story told.
In the night, hearts intertwine,
In dusk's embrace, love will shine.

The Weight of Togetherness

Hand in hand through life's vast maze,
We lift each other's heavy gaze.
In laughter shared, burdens reduce,
In shared silence, we find our roots.

Each moment built on trust and grace,
We find our strength in this embrace.
The weight we carry, soft and sweet,
With every heartbeat, we are complete.

Anchors of Belonging

In the harbor of our souls' ports,
Together we weather each storm's cohorts.
Roots grow deep in the land we share,
In the warmth of love, we rest and care.

With laughter that echoes in the air,
We gather moments, beyond compare.
In every glance, there's a spark,
Anchoring us through the dark.

The Art of Compromise

In the dance of give and take,
We mold like clay, for kindness' sake.
Words may clash, but hearts align,
In the middle ground, love will shine.

Like tides that ebb and flow in time,
We find our rhythm, soft as rhyme.
Every choice a step we make,
In this art, a bond we stake.

Fragile Tether

In the whisper of night,
Two hearts softly connect,
Bound by a fragile thread,
Holding love with respect.

Dancing in shadows' grace,
Afraid yet feeling bold,
Every moment they chase,
A story yet untold.

Trust fluttering like leaves,
Caught in a gentle breeze,
Fragile yet so alive,
A bond that seeks to please.

Through storms and through calm,
The tether may fray wide,
Yet love's tender balm,
Will heal where they confide.

In silence they vow strength,
To weather all that's thrown,
Such beauty in the length,
Of a love that is grown.

The Weight of Trust

A promise held so dear,
Can lift us to the sky,
Yet if it fades to fear,
The heart begins to sigh.

Like a stone in a stream,
Trust can shift and flow,
Reflecting every dream,
In light's warm golden glow.

But once it starts to crack,
The world seems to cave in,
Each word a memory's track,
A race we cannot win.

With careful, tender hands,
We build it brick by brick,
Forging our quiet stands,
Through moments soft and thick.

In the stillness of night,
We question and we give,
The weight of trust ignites,
A fire through which we live.

Embracing Paradox

In shadows lies the light,
In truth we find our dreams,
Balancing wrong and right,
Life's not as simple as it seems.

We seek joy in the pain,
Emotions whirl and blend,
In loss, there's always gain,
A cycle that won't end.

Laughter wraps around tears,
While time drips like a stream,
Chasing after our fears,
We learn to love the dream.

Holding tight to the mess,
The chaos of our days,
In the universe's dress,
We dance in tangled ways.

Here we stand in the flux,
With hearts both brave and meek,
Embracing paradox,
In every strong or weak.

The Scale of Friendship

A heart that knows you well,
Carries the weight of time,
In laughter and in hell,
Together we will climb.

Measured in moments shared,
In whispers soft and low,
Each challenge boldly dared,
In trust's vibrant flow.

The scales of give and take,
Are balanced with such care,
In sweet bond hearts awake,
Finding treasure rare.

With each secret confided,
Our souls begin to blend,
Through trials we abided,
Forces that won't bend.

In this delicate dance,
We weigh joy with our pain,
For friendship, given a chance,
Is sunlight through the rain.

Threading Ties

In the loom of life we spin,
Threads of laughter, love within.
Binding hearts, a gentle sway,
We weave our dreams in light of day.

Each knot a promise, firm and true,
Colors merging, me and you.
Silken bonds that cannot fray,
Together strong, come what may.

Through storms and trials, we will stand,
Hand in hand, we'll face the land.
With every twist, our spirits rise,
In the tapestry, hope never dies.

Time may test the strength we claim,
But in our hearts, we share one name.
As seasons change, our fabric grows,
In the warmth of love, our spirit glows.

In every thread, a story told,
Of cherished moments, brave and bold.
So let us weave, with love as guide,
In the fabric of life, we'll always bide.

Equilibrium of Hearts

In silence, we find a gentle beat,
Hearts in balance, softly greet.
A dance of knowing, eyes collide,
In whispered dreams, we confide.

The scales of trust, they gently sway,
Drawing closer, come what may.
Each moment shared, a precious art,
In the stillness, we find our heart.

Through the chaos, we will glide,
In harmony, we choose our stride.
With every pulse, the world aligns,
In this union, love defines.

Every heartbeat, a sacred song,
Two souls dancing, where they belong.
In laughter's echo, pain can part,
As we cherish the equilibrium of hearts.

With gentle hands, we craft our fate,
Sealing bonds that never wait.
In the orchestra of whispered dreams,
Together we'll soar on silver beams.

Weaving Connections

Threads of fate, intertwined tight,
Drawing us close, igniting light.
In every glance, a story starts,
A fabric rich, the art of hearts.

Through laughter shared and tears that fall,
We gather strength, we stand tall.
Each connection, a vibrant hue,
In this vast world, just me and you.

In every hug, warmth resides,
In friendship's cloak, love abides.
With open arms and minds attuned,
We find our place beneath the moon.

Through distance wide, our spirits soar,
Across the miles, forevermore.
In every thread, a bond refined,
In this weave, our hearts aligned.

So let us thread our lives with care,
With gentle hands and love to share.
In the tapestry of life we find,
True connections, forever entwined.

The Dance of Togetherness

In every step, we find our grace,
A rhythm shared, a warm embrace.
With laughter ringing, spirits soar,
In this dance, we ask for more.

We twirl through days, hand in hand,
In perfect sync, we take a stand.
Every move, a story spun,
In the dance of hearts, we are one.

Through highs and lows, we sway and spin,
In this ballet, we lose, we win.
With every glance, the world expands,
Together, united, in love's commands.

A waltz of dreams, both near and far,
Guided by hope, our shining star.
In every twirl, we lose our fears,
The dance of togetherness, through years.

So take my hand and let us glide,
In joy and sorrow, side by side.
In this dance of life, hearts align,
Together we shall always shine.

The Tension of Trust

In whispers shared and secrets kept,
A fragile bond where fears have slept.
Yet shadows lurk, as doubts persist,
In the silence of a lover's tryst.

Each promise made, a thread of hope,
Across the chasm, we learn to cope.
With every glance, the weight we share,
In the balance of the love we bear.

Through storms we weave, we twist and turn,
In lessons found, the hearts still learn.
Yet distance grows with every sigh,
In the spaces where trust might die.

Yet still we tread on paths unseen,
With every heartbeat, love's routine.
In the cracks, where sunlight bends,
We find the way, where trust transcends.

So here we stand, though torn apart,
A fragile dance within the heart.
In tension held, we find our place,
In trust renewed, we seek embrace.

Convergence of Souls

In a sea of stars, we drift alone,
Yet paths align, and hearts are shown.
At crossroads bright, our fates entwine,
In subtle glances, love's design.

With every beat, two rhythms blend,
A silent pact that cannot end.
Through whispered dreams, we chase the light,
In the darkness, souls take flight.

Our journeys echo, near and far,
A testament written in every scar.
Together we rise, through joy and pain,
In the tapestry, love's sweet refrain.

In moments fleeting, we find our song,
In chords of silence, where we belong.
Two spirits mingle, an unseen pull,
In this dance, our hearts are full.

As destinies merge, the world will see,
An endless love, just you and me.
In the convergence, we are whole,
A union bound, two wandering souls.

The Scale of Solace

In quiet moments, we seek the calm,
A fragile peace, a soothing balm.
With every thought, an ebb and flow,
In the depths, where solace grows.

Through shadows cast, our hearts align,
Each breath we take, a touch divine.
As we weigh the burdens, we find the gold,
In the stories of the brave and bold.

With gentle hands, we lift the weight,
From sorrow's grasp, we navigate.
In laughter's echo, pain finds rest,
In the journey, we are blessed.

As we measure joy in tender terms,
In the fires of love, the spirit learns.
Each tear a drop upon the scale,
In the dance of life, we will prevail.

So let us find, in every crack,
A glimpse of light, a warming track.
For in each moment, solace flows,
In the heart's embrace, true healing grows.

Dance of Dichotomy

In the twilight where shadows play,
Light and dark both find their way.
In contradictions, we find the beat,
In every challenge, we face defeat.

With each heartbeat, the push and pull,
In the chaos, our lives are full.
Joy and sorrow, hand in hand,
In the dance, we take a stand.

Life's grand tapestry weaves both threads,
In laughter's chords, where silence spreads.
Through every choice, we find the span,
In the web of fate, we understand.

So let us twirl in the vibrant night,
Embrace the struggle, chase the light.
For in this dance of what we know,
Both sides combined, we truly grow.

A beautiful mess, this life we lead,
In dualities, we plant the seed.
To cherish both, the ups and downs,
In the rhythm, love wears the crowns.

The Art of Together

In the quiet dusk we stand,
Two hearts beating hand in hand,
Whispers shared in soft embrace,
A world created in our space.

Colors blend, a vivid hue,
Every moment feels so new,
Laughter dances in the air,
Crafting memories we both share.

In the tapestry we weave,
Threads of hope, we truly believe,
Designs of dreams in every thread,
Creating paths where love is led.

Through storms that howl, we'll find our way,
Guided by the light of day,
Together we can face it all,
In every rise and every fall.

The Scale of Sentiment

In the realm of feelings deep,
Where secrets of the heart do seep,
Each smile weighs a thousand joys,
Silent sighs, our hopes deploys.

Measured moments, joy and pain,
The sunshine blends with the rain,
In every glance, a story told,
The warmth of solace we behold.

When sorrow wraps like heavy cloth,
We find strength in the quiet froth,
Compassion scales the peaks of trust,
In shared burdens, love is a must.

A balance struck between the two,
Each heart's whisper, soft and true,
Navigating through it all,
In love's embrace, we never fall.

Navigating Nuance

In the shades of gray we find,
Complexity within the mind,
Every thought, a layered tale,
In subtle cues, we will prevail.

Whispers dance like fleeting light,
A feeling sensed, yet out of sight,
In silent pauses, truths draw near,
Navigating all we hold dear.

With every word, a twist or turn,
Understanding's flame doth burn,
As we journey through the maze,
Connection blooms in subtle ways.

To see the beauty in the small,
In every rise, in every fall,
A gentle touch, a knowing glance,
In nuance, we find our chance.

Symmetry of Love

In perfect balance, we align,
Your heartbeat syncs with mine,
Echoes of a life we share,
In harmony, we find our care.

With every moment, closely knit,
A dance of souls, we never quit,
Two paths converge, a light entwined,
In unity, our hearts combined.

Around us, beauty all around,
In laughter's song, our joys abound,
In every struggle, side by side,
In love's embrace, we shall abide.

Together, we explore the vast,
A journey built to ever last,
In symmetry, our spirits soar,
Love's sweet balance, forevermore.

The Art of Togetherness

In every laugh, a shared delight,
In quiet moments, hearts ignite.
Hands entwined, two souls as one,
Together we shine like the sun.

Through storms we face, we find our way,
In every word, in what we say.
With every step, we share the load,
In unity, we write our ode.

Holding On

Fingers clasped, a warm embrace,
In your eyes, I find my place.
The world may change, but we stand firm,
In love's embrace, we shall not squirm.

Memories gathered, treasures worn,
Through turbulent times, new bonds are born.
With whispers soft, we share our fears,
In holding on, we conquer years.

Letting Go

A gentle breeze, a fading song,
The weight of past, no longer strong.
In the quiet night, we learn to sigh,
To release the chains that bind us high.

With every step, a heart set free,
In the silence, we find decree.
Embracing change, we face the dawn,
In letting go, we carry on.

The Ties that Anchor

In the depths of storms, we find our ground,
With steadfast love, our hearts are bound.
Through raging seas and endless night,
The ties that anchor hold us tight.

In laughter shared and burdens borne,
In every sunrise, hope is sworn.
Bound by dreams, we rise and flow,
In every heart, the love we sow.

In Sync with Silent Whispers

In quiet moments, secrets dance,
Two souls entwined, lost in a trance.
With silent words, our spirits speak,
In gentle starlight, we find the peak.

From whispered dreams to twilight's care,
In every glance, a truth we share.
With heartbeats matched, the world can see,
In sync with silence, we are free.

The Rhythm of Together

In the quiet of the night,
Hearts beat in gentle sync,
United by a soft light,
Drawing closer with each blink.

Hands entwined in warm embrace,
Every moment feels like gold,
In this sweet, familiar space,
Our stories gently told.

Laughter dances in the air,
Echoes of our shared delight,
Together, there's naught to compare,
In the rhythm, pure and right.

Side by side we face the dawn,
New adventures on the way,
With you, I feel I belong,
In this dance, come what may.

Through the valleys and the peaks,
We ride the waves of joy and pain,
In our hearts, love softly speaks,
The rhythm will remain.

Weaving Whispers

In the quiet, whispers flow,
Threads of dreams begin to weave,
Capturing moments, soft and slow,
Creating tales we both believe.

Softly spoken, secrets shared,
Woven into the fabric tight,
Every word, a promise bared,
Binding us in endless light.

Through the night, the stories grow,
In the spaces, silence hums,
With each heartbeat, feelings glow,
In this warmth, our love becomes.

Each glance exchanged tells a tale,
Invisible threads draw us near,
In this bond, we shall not pale,
Embraced in every whispered cheer.

As we weave, the world may fade,
In our tapestry, we're found,
In this intimacy we've made,
Our hearts forever bound.

The Duality of Distance

Miles apart, yet close at hand,
In every thought, you reside,
Bridges built upon the sand,
In dreams, it's you I confide.

The moonlight dances on the sea,
Reflecting both loss and grace,
In every wave, I feel you near,
In every sunset, your embrace.

Distance teaches hearts to yearn,
Fuels a fire deep inside,
In the silence, we discern,
Love's unyielding, endless tide.

Though the path may twist and bend,
Our spirits soar across the void,
In this journey, we transcend,
In each moment, love enjoyed.

So here we stand, two hearts apart,
Yet woven tight, you and I,
With every beat, an artful start,
In distance, love will never die.

Poise in Togetherness

In the stillness of the morn,
We find solace in our place,
With the rising sun reborn,
Love's reflection on each face.

Harmony in every glance,
Moments flowing, time stands still,
In your eyes, a gentle dance,
In our hearts, a shared thrill.

When the storms begin to roll,
Hand in hand, we won't divide,
In your strength, I find my soul,
Together, we will always bide.

Each breath we take, a gentle pause,
In the chaos, we find peace,
In our bond, a tender cause,
From this love, we never cease.

In the art of being one,
We create a world so bright,
Underneath the vast, wide sun,
Poise in love, our guiding light.

Navigating the Space Between

In shadows where silence dwells,
We whisper dreams, break our shells.
Each step forward, hand in hand,
Together we choose to stand.

Through valleys deep and hills so high,
We navigate beneath the sky.
With hearts aligned, we chart the way,
Creating light in shades of gray.

In moments lost, we find our grace,
A dance of trust in this shared space.
Though paths may twist and turn anew,
In every challenge, I find you.

With courage strong, we face the dawn,
In unity, the fears we've drawn.
For in the gap, love shines so bright,
Connecting us with guiding light.

So here we are, two souls entwined,
In spaces rich, our fates designed.
Together we'll weather any storm,
In every challenge, we transform.

Threads of Togetherness

In every thread, a story we weave,
Through laughter shared and moments we cleave.
Each strand connects, a bond so tight,
In the tapestry of day and night.

With colors bright, we paint our days,
In shades of joy, in faithful ways.
Though seasons shift and winds may blow,
Our threads remain, they ebb and flow.

In heartbeats shared, our lives align,
In whispered hopes, our thoughts combine.
We hold each other, spirits free,
Together strong, in unity.

Through storms we brave, through calm we glide,
In every leap, we stand with pride.
For in the weave, our spirits rise,
In threads of love, we touch the skies.

So let us stitch this quilt of grace,
With every moment we embrace.
Through threads of gold, our lives will dance,
In the art of togetherness, we take our chance.

The Spectrum of Support

In vibrant hues, we paint the day,
With hands to lift, we find our way.
Each color bright, a song, a sound,
In unity, we're always found.

Through highs and lows, we share the load,
In gentle words, our love bestowed.
With open hearts, we light the night,
Together, we'll keep hope in sight.

In every shade, a different role,
Supportive arms for every soul.
Through shadows cast, we shine so clear,
In every heartbeat, we draw near.

As rainbows arch above the gloom,
In every challenge, we find room.
To grow, to learn, to stand as one,
In every struggle, we have won.

So let us be a guiding light,
In every dark, we spark the bright.
For in the spectrum, we are strong,
In support's embrace, we all belong.

In Rhythm with Each Other

In gentle beats, our hearts align,
With every step, the world is fine.
In sync we move, like waves at sea,
In rhythm's grace, just you and me.

With every note, we find our way,
In melodies that softly play.
Through trials faced and joys expressed,
In harmony, we are blessed.

When silence falls, we understand,
The music lives in touch and hand.
In every pause, our souls connect,
In every breath, we find respect.

With laughter bright, we lift the day,
In echoed dreams, we choose to stay.
For in this dance, our spirits soar,
In rhythm's pulse, we yearn for more.

So let our hearts beat strong and true,
In every step, I find in you.
Together we'll embrace the song,
In rhythm with each other, we belong.

A Bridge of Souls

In twilight's glow, we find our way,
Threads of light that softly sway.
Each whispered dream, a gentle call,
Together, we rise, never to fall.

Hand in hand, through storms we tread,
A sturdy bridge where hearts are led.
Bound by hope, we cross the night,
Finding warmth in shared light.

With every laugh, with every tear,
We build a bond that conquers fear.
Across the chasm, thoughts entwine,
In this embrace, your soul is mine.

In shadows cast, we still can shine,
A dance of spirits, yours and mine.
Through every trial, we shall prevail,
Together, we weave our tale.

So let us walk this bridge of fate,
In unity, we celebrate.
For in the depths, our spirits soar,
A bridge of souls, forevermore.

Symphonic Relationships

In the symphony of heart's embrace,
Each note we play finds its place.
Melodies blend, harmonies grow,
In this dance, our feelings flow.

Like crescendos reaching high,
We rise together, touch the sky.
With gentle whispers, bold refrains,
We navigate through joys and pains.

Each silence speaks in tender ways,
A cadence felt in softer days.
In every chord, a tale unfolds,
Of passion deep and love untold.

Through time's passage, the music plays,
In varied rhythms, our hearts blaze.
From all the notes, a song is spun,
In this symphony, we are one.

So let us dance in life's embrace,
In every moment, find our space.
For in this symphonic journey,
Our hearts will sing in harmony.

Unity in Diversity

In fields of color, blooms array,
Each petal tells a different way.
Together they thrive, side by side,
In unity, our hearts confide.

From whispers soft to loud refrains,
We learn through joy, we learn through pains.
One voice rises, a call for peace,
In diversity, our love won't cease.

Like rivers merge in ocean's sway,
Cultures blend, a rich display.
With every heartbeat, every smile,
We break the barriers, mile by mile.

Together we journey, hand in hand,
Embracing tales from every land.
In shared moments, we redefine,
What it means to truly shine.

So let us celebrate the myriad hues,
In diversity, we find our muse.
For in this world, so vast and wide,
Unity flourishes, side by side.

Echoes of Affinity

In the silence, how heartbeats share,
Echoes linger in gentle air.
With every glance, a spark ignites,
A bond so deep, it breaks the nights.

Across the distance, thoughts align,
In hidden corners, souls entwine.
With tender whispers lost in time,
We find meaning in love's rhyme.

Through laughter shared and secrets told,
In echoes bright, our dreams unfold.
In shadows cast beneath the moon,
Our hearts sing softly, a sweet tune.

Every memory leaves a trace,
In every moment, our hearts race.
In every choice, affinity grows,
In this journey, love bestows.

So let the echoes guide our way,
As stars will light the night to day.
For in this symphony of fate,
We find the love that can't abate.

Threads of Connection

In the fabric of life, we weave,
Threads of laughter, hopes, and dreams.
Each strand a story, a gentle reprieve,
Binding our hearts, or so it seems.

In quiet moments, we share our fears,
Tangled together, through joy and strife.
Through the distance, through the years,
These threads hold strong, the essence of life.

A tapestry rich, with colors bright,
Every encounter, a mark in time.
We celebrate love, a radiant light,
In every heartbeat, a sweet rhyme.

Frayed edges tell of battles won,
While soft places comfort, heal our woes.
Together we shine, like the morning sun,
In the threads of connection, our love grows.

So let us stitch memories, thread by thread,
Crafting a legacy, woven and strong.
In this dance of life, we're gently led,
Together forever, where we belong.

The Scale of Affection

In a balance of hearts, we find our way,
Measuring kindness, in myriad forms.
With each gentle gesture, we sway,
In love's embrace, as life transforms.

Like a feather, light on the breeze,
Tender moments weigh more than gold.
With every smile, a heart's reprise,
The scale of affection, a story told.

In storms we weather, we stand as one,
The burden shared, no longer alone.
Through laughter and tears, our battles won,
In the scale of affection, our love has grown.

Each whisper's weight in quiet night,
Transcends the ledger, where love abides.
Together we shine, forever bright,
In the scale of affection, trust resides.

So let us measure with every glance,
The moments we share, the paths we roam.
In the dance of affection, we find our chance,
To scale the heights, as we make it home.

Harmony at Heart's Edge

In twilight's glow, we lean and sway,
Heartbeat to heartbeat, a rhythmic embrace.
In silence, we find what words can't say,
Harmony's tune, a sacred space.

With whispers soft, we tread the line,
Between dreams shared, and fears that rise.
In the clash of worlds, our souls align,
Creating a symphony beneath the skies.

Like waves that crash, yet dance in time,
Our hearts beat steady, in perfect sync.
In every note, in every rhyme,
We find the colors, the missing link.

Around the edge, where shadows dwell,
Hope flickers bright, like stars above.
In harmony's grip, all will be well,
For in this space, we find our love.

So let us embrace, as day meets night,
In the heart's quiet edge, where dreams unite.
With every heartbeat, we take our flight,
In harmony's song, we find our light.

Weighing Ties

In the balance of life, we weigh our ties,
With each choice, a heart's plea.
Through laughter shared, through whispered sighs,
In the depths of love, we find the key.

Count the moments, both bitter and sweet,
Each memory etched, a page in time.
In the tapestry woven, our lives repeat,
Weighing the ties, a dance so sublime.

A gentle touch, a knowing glance,
The gravity pulls, in softest ways.
In the weight of love, there's no chance,
For bonds to break, through darkened days.

Side by side, in storms we face,
With anchored hearts, we brave the tide.
For weighing ties, in love's embrace,
We find our strength, where dreams reside.

So let us cherish this fragile bond,
In every heartbeat, let's find our way.
With each promise made, our hearts respond,
In the weighing of ties, we choose to stay.

Steadying Each Step

With every footfall, I find my ground,
Embracing the rhythm, a soothing sound.
The path may waver, but I hold the line,
In the stillness of moments, I know I'm fine.

Glimmers of doubt may cross my mind,
Yet courage whispers, 'You're one of a kind.'
In shadows and light, I tread with care,
Each step a dance, a breath of air.

Through trials faced, my spirit grows,
Rooted in purpose, a river flows.
Emboldened by love, I rise anew,
With every heartbeat, I pursue the true.

In the storm's embrace, I hold my stance,
Navigating through life's wild dance.
With grace I conquer, with strength I roam,
Each step reminding me, I'm never alone.

The Equinox of Connection

When day and night hold hands so tight,
A balance forged in gentle light.
In equal measure, we share our dreams,
Our hearts entwined like flowing streams.

With whispered truths that bridge the space,
A sacred bond in this shared place.
On this equinox, let's weave our song,
In harmony found, where we belong.

The ebb and flow of life's design,
Bringing souls together, yours and mine.
In moments small, a timeless touch,
We find the beauty in caring much.

Let laughter echo in the air,
As we weave stories, love to share.
In twilight's glow, let spirits soar,
Connected forever, forevermore.

The Flow of Unity

In the river of life, we find our way,
Current strong, come what may.
Currents of purpose, love's embrace,
Together we journey, a sacred space.

As tides rise and fall, we stand as one,
Under the moon, beneath the sun.
Dancing together, a timeless trance,
In the flow of unity, we take our chance.

Voices blend in a harmony sweet,
In every heartbeat, our souls meet.
With every splash of joy and grace,
We navigate life's beautiful race.

Through valleys deep and mountains high,
We hold each other, never to shy.
In togetherness, our dreams ignite,
In the flow of unity, we shine bright.

Hearts in Tandem

Two hearts beating, a rhythmic song,
In perfect harmony, where we belong.
With every glance, a story told,
In love's embrace, we grow bold.

Side by side, we face the day,
In laughter and tears, come what may.
With hands entwined, we walk this path,
Finding joy in each other's laugh.

In moments shared, we find our light,
Guiding each other through the night.
With every whisper, a promise made,
In every challenge, together we wade.

Through storms that rage and skies so clear,
Our hearts in tandem, ever near.
In every heartbeat, love's refrain,
Together we thrive, through joy and pain.

The Fabric of Bonds

Threads of laughter weave the air,
In shared moments, we find care.
Each smile stitches joy and trust,
In our embrace, it's love we thrust.

Woven tightly, never frayed,
In the warmth, our fears allayed.
Patterns of life, forever sewn,
In every stitch, our hearts have grown.

The fabric holds our whispered dreams,
In every tear, the sunlight beams.
Together, we are stitched as one,
Through every rift, our threads outrun.

Colors blend, a vibrant scheme,
In this tapestry, we dare to dream.
Bound by love and gentle grace,
In this fabric, our hearts find place.

Stitch by stitch, we craft our fate,
In every loop, we resonate.
Yet through the storms, we will stand fast,
The fabric of bonds unsurpassed.

Weightlessness in Closeness

In the quiet, hearts collide,
Every heartbeat, a gentle tide.
Gravity falls, we rise above,
Weightless, lost in tender love.

Soft whispers float in the night,
In each breath, we find our light.
Moments stretch, time drifts away,
In this closeness, we choose to stay.

Floating dreams, like leaves in air,
A dance of souls, a cosmic pair.
Embracing the void, we are free,
In weightlessness, just you and me.

Each glance shared, an endless flight,
In your arms, everything feels right.
We defy the world, with no strings,
In love's weightless light, we have wings.

Our hearts soar high, unbound, unfurled,
In this dream, we create our world.
With every moment, we learn and grow,
In weightlessness, our love will flow.

The Intersection of Hearts

Two paths converge, a fated place,
In the twilight, we find our grace.
Hearts aligned, a perfect view,
In this moment, it's me and you.

Echoes linger in the air,
In silence, I feel you there.
Where dreams meet, our spirits dance,
In this intersection, we take a chance.

Crossroads marked by love's embrace,
In every glance, a warm trace.
Winding roads, yet here we stand,
Together, we sculpt this land.

The sun dips low, our shadows blend,
In this journey, we will transcend.
In every heartbeat, in every sign,
At this intersection, you are mine.

Always together, through twists unknown,
In our hearts, a seed is grown.
We chart the course, with love impart,
In this intersection, we will start.

Gentle Pulls

Like the tide that pulls the shore,
You draw me in, I want you more.
With every smile, a gentle tug,
In a world so vast, it's you I hug.

Invisible threads bind us tight,
In every whisper, we find light.
A dance that flows, soft yet sure,
In gentle pulls, my heart is pure.

Like the moon that guides the sea,
You call to me, a mystery.
Through the depths, our souls will glide,
In gentle pulls, I'll be your guide.

A tender breeze, a soft caress,
In your presence, I find rest.
With every heartbeat, close and near,
In gentle pulls, I'll hold you dear.

Two magnets drawn, we can't resist,
In this journey, love persists.
Through life's storms, we find our way,
In gentle pulls, forever stay.

Heartbeats in Sync

In the quiet of the night,
Two hearts whisper low,
A rhythm so alive,
In soft starlight's glow.

Fingers intertwined tight,
Promises softly spoken,
Every glance ignites fire,
Our bond never broken.

Time stands still for us,
As echoes of our dreams,
We sway to love's sweet song,
In perfect harmony's beams.

With every breath we share,
A symphony unfolds,
In the dance of our souls,
A tale forever told.

We drift through life as one,
Unfazed by what may come,
Heartbeats in sync, we roam,
In love's sacred kingdom.

The Give and Take

In the ebb and flow of days,
We learn the art of trust,
In laughter and in tears,
Together we adjust.

Moments shared and traded,
A balance we embrace,
Each kindness we hand off,
In love's gentle grace.

When shadows loom above,
We stand side by side,
The give and take of hearts,
Our ever-rolling tide.

Through storms that come our way,
We find our strength anew,
In the sanctuary found,
In me and you.

The world may shift and change,
But this truth remains,
In the give and take of love,
Our spirit always gains.

Ties that Bind and Bend

Roots entwined beneath,
Two souls find their way,
In this dance of life,
Together we shall sway.

Every moment captured,
In laughter and in fright,
These ties that bind us close,
Are forged in darkest night.

When paths grow rough and wild,
We flex but do not break,
In the trials that we've faced,
Each bond's a choice we make.

Through every twist and turn,
We navigate the bends,
In the fabric of our days,
Love's thread never ends.

So let the storms roll in,
Together, we'll defend,
For in our hearts, we know,
These ties shall never end.

Shifting Shadows

In the twilight's embrace,
Shadows dance and glide,
Whispering tales of old,
Where mysteries reside.

With every passing hour,
Shapes begin to blur,
In the soft, fading light,
What is real, we prefer.

The world turned upside down,
In a fleeting glance,
With every heartbeat felt,
We join in shadow's dance.

Yet within this duality,
Hope flickers like a flame,
In the darkest corners found,
We still rise, unashamed.

So let the shadows shift,
Let the night take its hold,
For in this fleeting play,
Our stories shall be told.

Chords of Companionship

In the silence, hearts entwine,
Melodies of friendship shine.
Through laughter, tears, we stand,
With each note, hand in hand.

Whispers shared beneath the stars,
Healing wounds, erasing scars.
A symphony of trust we play,
In each chord, we find our way.

Through the storms that come our way,
Side by side, we choose to stay.
With every heartbeat, strong and true,
Our song grows deeper, just me and you.

As seasons change and time will bend,
Our harmony will never end.
In every struggle, we'll unite,
Chords of companionship, pure light.

Together we can face the night,
In the darkness, we ignite.
A duet of souls, forever bright,
In the music, love takes flight.

Dancing on a Tightrope

Step by step, we find our way,
Balancing what words can't say.
In the air, our fears dissolve,
Together, all problems resolve.

With each sway and gentle turn,
Our passion, like a candle, burns.
Facing the void, hand in hand,
For balance, together we stand.

Winds may howl and shadows loom,
Yet we dance, dispelling gloom.
Trusting in the rhythm's call,
In this dance, we will not fall.

And when the world begins to spin,
Together in laughter, we begin.
Through the highs and through the lows,
Our bond, like a river, flows.

So let us twirl on this fragile line,
With hearts entwined, our souls combine.
Life's a dance, both fierce and free,
On this tightrope, just you and me.

Embracing the Equinox

As day meets night, we find our space,
In quietude, a warm embrace.
Nature whispers, soft and sweet,
Two worlds converge, a dance complete.

Golden hues and shadows blend,
Life's rhythms twist, but never end.
In balance, the sun and moon,
Together, they'll hum a lullaby tune.

Leaves will fall, yet blooms will rise,
In this moment, we touch the skies.
Each heartbeat echoes, strong and clear,
In the equinox, we draw near.

So let us bask in twilight's glow,
With every moment, let love flow.
In the stillness, hand in hand,
We'll cherish this equal land.

Embracing change, we'll learn to live,
In each season, love we give.
A journey shared, we intertwine,
In the embrace of the divine.

When Worlds Align

Two paths converge beneath the stars,
Bringing together, near and far.
In the cosmos, fate draws near,
When worlds align, the vision's clear.

Hearts like planets, spinning bright,
Creating magic in the night.
With gravity's pull, we are bound,
In this union, love is found.

Dreams collide, illuminating skies,
In the stillness, our spirits rise.
Timeless dance of chance and choice,
In this moment, we find our voice.

With every glance and every sigh,
We break the limits, reach for high.
In the union, rivers flow,
When worlds align, we surely glow.

Together through life's twisting maze,
In this wonder, we lose our gaze.
For in the light where hearts enshrine,
Forever blessed when worlds align.

When Ties Find Flow

In moments still, the world can pause,
A rush of ties, a gentle cause.
Through whispered dreams, they intertwine,
A dance of souls, in perfect line.

With every glance, a spark ignites,
An unseen bond that softly bites.
Together now, they forge their way,
As night gives in to breaking day.

Through winding paths, their spirits soar,
In unity, they seek for more.
With open hearts, they bravely tread,
A journey shared, where love is spread.

When shadows loom and doubts arise,
They grasp the light, beyond the skies.
For in their flow, the ties will mend,
A story told, that has no end.

A Unified Compass

In the quiet space where dreams align,
A compass spins, both yours and mine.
Together we navigate the night,
Trusting the stars to guide our flight.

Every heartbeat, a rhythmic call,
Hand in hand, we won't let fall.
With every breath, we find the way,
In unity, come what may.

The map of hearts, forever drawn,
A tapestry from dusk to dawn.
Through stormy seas or tranquil shores,
Our compass points to love once more.

Each moment shared, a lesson learned,
In patience, love can be returned.
With steadfast hearts, we roam so free,
The pull of trust, our destiny.

Tethered Hearts

Across the void, two hearts collide,
In silent currents, love will guide.
With each connection, fate designs,
A tethered truth, where hope aligns.

In laughter's echo, joy takes flight,
In tenderness, they hold on tight.
Through trials faced, their strength does bloom,
A garden rich dispelling gloom.

With whispered dreams beneath the night,
Together they bask in soft twilight.
Each heartbeat sings their secret song,
In harmony, where they belong.

No matter distance, space or time,
These tethered hearts will always climb.
With every struggle, they will find,
A deeper bond that leaves none blind.

Equilibrium in Embrace

In morning still, two souls entwined,
An embrace that feels like home, defined.
With gentle hands, the weight is shared,
In balance found, no need for care.

As twilight fades, they weave a thread,
Of whispered hopes that gently spread.
With every pause, they find their grace,
In simple joy, in love's embrace.

Each challenge met, they stand as one,
In perfect rhythm, they have won.
Through ebb and flow of time and space,
They find their strength in sweet embrace.

With every heartbeat, calmness made,
In unity, no fears invade.
For in this dance, they lift and sway,
Equilibrium, day by day.

Navigating Nuances

In a world of shades and gray,
We dance on paths, unsure to stay.
Each choice a whisper, soft and light,
Guiding us through the dimmest night.

Layers unfold, secrets to find,
Seeking clarity in the blind.
With every step, a lesson learned,
In the heart's fire, a passion burned.

Words may shift like the evening breeze,
Truths tucked away with artful ease.
Understanding creeps like dawn's first ray,
Illuminating the hidden way.

We navigate these winding streets,
Where voices blend and silence meets.
With open arms and hearts so true,
We carve our path, both old and new.

Embrace the gray, for therein lies,
The beauty seen through watchful eyes.
In nuances, we find our grace,
A journey shared in this vast space.

The Balance of Giving

In the dance of hands, we share,
Gifts of kindness, light as air.
With open hearts, we start to weave,
A tapestry of love to believe.

Yet in this flow, let's not forget,
To nurture self with no regret.
For giving well means growing too,
A bloom that thrives in morning dew.

Each gesture small, yet full of grace,
Reflects the warmth in every space.
Balance found in the heart's delight,
Turning darkness into light.

A smile shared can bridge the gap,
Compassion found in a gentle clap.
Together we rise, hands intertwined,
In the rhythm of love, we find.

As we give, let love return,
In this dance, our hearts shall burn.
In the balance, we learn to be,
Both givers and receivers, you and me.

Equilibrium in Emotion

In the heart's realm, storms may sway,
Feelings ebbing night and day.
We seek the calm through tides that rise,
To find our peace beneath the skies.

Joy dances lightly, shadows may creep,
In the balance, our secrets keep.
From laughter's burst to sorrow's sigh,
We learn to breathe, to question why.

Each emotion a thread, finely spun,
Connecting us till day is done.
In the weave of feelings, truth unfolds,
A story told as life beholds.

With every tear, we wash the pain,
In joy's embrace, we start again.
A symphony of highs and lows,
In tender equilibrium, love grows.

So let us dance through joy and strife,
Embracing the colors of our life.
In the balance, we find our way,
In emotion's world, we'll choose to stay.

Walking the Tightrope of Care

With careful steps, we walk the line,
Between duty's call and hearts that shine.
In the balance of love and heed,
We tread the path, fulfilling need.

Each moment weighs with choice profound,
In the silence, our hopes resound.
Support and strength, a sturdy bridge,
Mindful as we walk the ridge.

A gentle word, a listening ear,
In the tightrope dance, we stay near.
With every act of hold and sway,
We show the way, we light the day.

Yet let us pause, reflect on self,
Nurturing souls beyond the shelf.
For in our care, we often find,
The strength to lift the tied-up mind.

So let us walk this shared domain,
With open hearts, through joy and pain.
In tightrope dance, we learn and share,
The beauty found in simple care.

The Gentle Tug

A whisper in the breeze, so light,
Pulls at the heart, day and night.
Soft as a feather, it softly sways,
Guiding our dreams in delicate ways.

Each gentle tug, a hidden sign,
Connecting souls, your hand in mine.
Like threads of silk, a woven fate,
Drawn together, we await.

In quiet moments, feelings bloom,
A tender longing, dispelling gloom.
Through tides of time, we ebb and flow,
In love's embrace, we both can grow.

As stars align in the midnight sky,
The gentle tug reminds us why.
In every heartbeat, a dance shall rise,
Forever bound beneath these skies.

So let us cherish this softest pull,
Embracing the love that makes us whole.
With every tug, our spirits soar,
Together, always, forevermore.

A Delicate Balance

In the dance of light and shade,
We seek the truth that won't ever fade.
A fragile line we tread with care,
Striving to find the beauty there.

With heart and mind in constant sway,
We weigh the night against the day.
In laughter's echo, in silence deep,
A delicate balance, ours to keep.

Between the joy and the quiet pain,
In sunshine's glow and the soft rain.
Each heartbeat echoes, a rhythm fine,
In the space where love and hope align.

With every choice, a path we tread,
In the web of dreams that we have spread.
Finding grace in imperfections true,
A delicate balance made for two.

So let us dance upon this thread,
With faith in what lies just ahead.
In each moment, let our spirits shine,
For in our balance, love's design.

Finding the Center

In a whirlwind of thoughts, I seek,
A quiet place where I can speak.
A sanctuary within my mind,
Where solace waits, and peace I find.

Amidst the chaos, a still small voice,
Guiding my heart to make the choice.
To breathe in deep and simply be,
In this moment, I am free.

Like ripples spreading across a pond,
The center holds a magic bond.
Embracing stillness, fears subside,
In the heart's embrace, I confide.

I gather strength from what I feel,
In the quiet moments, I can heal.
With every breath, I find my way,
To the center of night and day.

In unity with the world around,
I find my voice, my purpose found.
To cherish life and all its grace,
Finding the center, my sacred space.

The Interplay of Intimacy

In the soft glow of twilight's kiss,
We dance together, lost in bliss.
A knowing glance, a gentle touch,
In the interplay, we find so much.

Words may falter, yet hearts can speak,
In whispered secrets, we feel unique.
Each shared moment, a thread we weave,
In this tapestry of love, we believe.

Through laughter's echo and tears that flow,
We navigate the highs and lows.
In the depth of trust, we will unfold,
The stories of us, forever told.

With every heartbeat, a symphony plays,
A melody formed in countless ways.
In the silent spaces, connection grows,
In the interplay, our love bestows.

So let us cherish this bond so rare,
In each embrace, a sacred care.
For in the dance of you and me,
Lies the beauty of intimacy.

Threads of Fate

In whispers soft, the threads entwine,
A tapestry of dreams, so fine.
Each knot a moment, spun with care,
In twilight's glow, we find our share.

Paths cross and weave in shadowed light,
Casting hopes into the night.
With every tug, a story grows,
In the fabric, life bestows.

Fate dances lightly, never still,
We follow, guided by will.
With every stitch, a promise made,
In this dance, we won't evade.

Among the threads, we laugh and cry,
In every tear, we learn to fly.
Together strong, we face the test,
In this bond, we find our rest.

The patterns shift, as seasons change,
In love's embrace, we rearrange.
Through tangled paths, we find our way,
In threads of fate, we choose to stay.

Embracing Complexity

In layers deep, the world unfolds,
A dance of truths, both brave and bold.
With every shadow, light will play,
In chaos found, we find our way.

The heart beats fast, yet slows with grace,
In every corner, a hidden space.
We navigate the twists and turns,
In every lesson, wisdom burns.

Embracing flaws, we learn to trust,
In the messy bits, we find what's just.
Through tangled thoughts, connections bloom,
In vibrant hues, we chase the gloom.

The stories told in fractured lines,
Reveal our hopes and old designs.
With every step, we grow aware,
In complexity, we learn to dare.

So let us dance in shades of grey,
Embracing life in every way.
For in the chaos, beauty sings,
A symphony of all our things.

The Space We Share

In quiet moments, silence speaks,
In every glance, affection peaks.
The space between us, soft and warm,
A gentle pull, our hearts conform.

Fingers brush past, electric spark,
In shared glances, we leave our mark.
In laughter's echo, time stands still,
In this embrace, we find our thrill.

The whispers loom in hallowed air,
In every heartbeat, we declare.
Together forged, we make our stand,
In the void, we understand.

Like constellations in the night,
We map our dreams in shared delight.
In this expanse, we learn to dream,
The depth of love, a flowing stream.

So let us linger, hearts laid bare,
In the sacred space, we choose to share.
For in this journey, side by side,
In timeless bond, we will abide.

Balancing the Weight of Us

On delicate lines, we tread with care,
In this dance, our burdens share.
With every step, we rise and fall,
In harmony, we hear love's call.

Through storms that rage, we hold on tight,
In shadowed paths, we seek the light.
With trust and faith, we face the tide,
In each other, we will abide.

In laughter's grace, the weight feels light,
In shared dreams, we take to flight.
With open hearts, we bear the load,
In this journey, love's our road.

With every challenge, we grow strong,
In tangled paths, we find our song.
In moments fleeting, time will bend,
Through every trial, love transcends.

So let us balance, hand in hand,
In this beautiful, fragile land.
For in the weight of us, we find,
A love that's lasting, intertwined.

Anchors in the Storm

In the darkest nights, we stand tall,
Holding tight, we won't let fall.
With anchors firm, we brave the sea,
Together we strong, just you and me.

Waves may crash, they may howl,
But in your eyes, I see the prowl.
A steadfast heart against the tide,
In the tempest, you're my guide.

Lightning flashes, fear draws near,
Yet with your voice, I lose the fear.
With every storm, we find our way,
In the chaos, we choose to stay.

Every gust tries to break apart,
Yet we're woven, heart to heart.
As the world churns, we remain,
Anchors steady, through the pain.

Together we face the raging storm,
Finding solace in love's warm.
In the end, it's you and I,
Anchored deep, 'neath stormy sky.

Harmony in the Tides

In the ebb and flow, we find a beat,
With gentle murmurs, our hearts meet.
Rhythm of waves, serene and calm,
Together we sing, a soothing psalm.

Whispers of the sea call our names,
Crafting memories, stoking flames.
In every rise, in every fall,
Harmony reigns, we answer the call.

The moon dances, its light aglow,
Casting dreams on the tides below.
In this embrace, we drift and glide,
Lost in the magic, side by side.

Every splash tells a tale so sweet,
With every heartbeat, we feel complete.
In this rhythm, our spirits soar,
Harmony whispers, forevermore.

As the tides shift, so do we learn,
In the flow of love, our passions burn.
In the dance of life, we intertwine,
In harmony's grace, our souls align.

The Weight of Affection

Like mountains high, our love stands bold,
A treasure rare, more precious than gold.
In every glance, the weight we share,
In quiet moments, a love laid bare.

Through valleys deep, and rivers wide,
Together we walk, side by side.
In laughter shared and tears we weep,
The weight of affection runs rich and deep.

With each embrace, the world fades away,
In your warmth, I long to stay.
In silence, we speak, a language clear,
The weight of love, forever near.

As seasons change, time shifts the hues,
In every choice, it's you I choose.
In tender moments, in strength so rare,
The weight of affection is ours to bear.

Through trials faced and dreams yet spun,
In unity, we come undone.
Together we rise, high above,
The weight we carry is only love.

Strands of Trust

In the delicate web of hearts entwined,
Strands of trust are redefined.
With every whisper, every sigh,
We weave a bond that will not die.

Through trials faced and storms unknown,
In this tapestry, our strength has grown.
Each thread a promise, each knot our vow,
In the fabric of love, we're woven now.

In quiet moments, we find our place,
In the depth of trust, we share our grace.
Together we stand, through thick and thin,
In strands of trust, our journey begins.

With open hearts, we face the fears,
In laughter shared, and in quiet tears.
Each strand a story, a path we trace,
In the journey of love, we find our space.

As the world turns, and shadows play,
Our strands of trust will light the way.
In every heartbeat, in every dream,
Together we flourish, a radiant beam.

Balancing the Scale of Love

In the quiet moments, we stand still,
Every heartbeat echoes, a whispered thrill.
Two souls entwined, in give and take,
A dance of trust, for love's sweet sake.

In laughter and tears, we find our way,
Through storms and sunshine, come what may.
A scale that shifts with every gaze,
In love's embrace, our spirits blaze.

With wings we soar, yet roots hold tight,
In balance we grow, from day to night.
Each tender gesture, a weightless sign,
In harmony's glow, our hearts align.

Facing the world, hand in hand,
Two hearts united, we beautifully stand.
With every challenge, we rise above,
In the gentle sway of the scale of love.

Together we build, a future bright,
In the depths of each other, we find our light.
With every heartbeat, a promise made,
In the balance of love, we're never afraid.

Intersecting Journeys

Two paths converge beneath the sky,
Where dreams are woven, and spirits fly.
In whispers of fate, our stories blend,
With every encounter, a chance to mend.

Mountains and valleys, we travel far,
Guided by hope, like a shining star.
In laughter and lessons, we share our way,
The beauty of life in each bold display.

With every step, we learn and grow,
Through trials faced, our strength will show.
A tapestry rich, with colors bright,
In intersecting journeys, we find our light.

From city streets to nature's peace,
In every moment, our worries cease.
Together we wander, in search of more,
With open hearts, we explore and soar.

As seasons shift, we cherish the ride,
In every heartbeat, we walk side by side.
With dreams unfolding, we pave our path,
In intersecting journeys, we find our laugh.

The Embrace of Differences

In the colors of life, we find our hue,
Different shades, yet harmoniously true.
Each story unique, a voice to share,
In the embrace of differences, we learn to care.

With open arms, we greet the unknown,
In the strength of contrasts, we have grown.
Through laughter and pain, we bridge the gap,
In every heartbeat, we weave our map.

In the symphony of voices, we hear a song,
In diverse rhythms, we all belong.
Celebrating each other, our hearts entwine,
In the beauty of differences, love will shine.

Through every struggle, we rise and fight,
In unity found, we claim our right.
With dignity shared, our spirits soar,
In the embrace of differences, we reach for more.

Together we flourish, hand in hand,
In a world that's vibrant, forever grand.
With each cherished moment, we paint our way,
In the embrace of differences, we find our day.

Pulling and Pushing

In every push, a chance to grow,
In gentle pulls, the love we sow.
A dance of force, of give and take,
In the balance of hearts, we choose to make.

With every tug, a lesson learned,
In the whispers of love, our passions burned.
Through trials faced, we find our strength,
In the pull and push, we go the length.

In moments of doubt, we stand our ground,
Through ebb and flow, our souls are bound.
With every challenge, we rise above,
In the pulling and pushing, we find our love.

As seasons change, we adapt with grace,
In the push of time, we find our place.
Together we navigate this winding road,
With every stress, our love is the code.

In the ebbing tide, we find the peace,
Through pulling and pushing, our hearts release.
In the dance of life, together we strive,
In the balance of love, we always thrive.

Tidal Movements of Affection

In the quiet of the night,
Waves whisper secrets near and far.
Hearts rise with the moon's glow,
Tides pull, each beat a star.

Soft breezes carry warm sighs,
The ocean dances in the dark.
Every ebb, a gentle goodbye,
Each flow, love's unwavering spark.

Shells scattered on sandy shores,
Echoes of laughter and tears.
Like the sea, love endures,
Waves brushing away our fears.

As currents shift and align,
Our souls drift in unison.
Hand in hand, we intertwine,
Navigating the world's horizon.

Through storms that may set us adrift,
We anchor deep, weathering time.
In love's sea, we often lift,
On tidal waves, together we climb.

Between the Lines of Love

Pages turn with a gentle grace,
Words woven in a hidden thread.
In whispers found in every space,
Love writes what the heart has said.

Between the lines, a spark ignites,
Silent vows, soft and sincere.
In every pause, in every bite,
Our story unfolds, crystal clear.

Ink stains mark our cherished past,
Lessons learned, faith ever bold.
In shadows deep, our hearts contrast,
Together, our future unfolds.

Each stanza a moment we've made,
Verses filled with laughter and dreams.
The tempo of love will not fade,
In the silence, it often gleams.

So let us write with honest hearts,
A tale bound by trust and cheer.
In each chapter, new love imparts,
Between the lines, you are near.

The Compass of Together

With laughter guiding our shared way,
A compass pointing true and clear.
In every dawn, we find our play,
Our hearts unite, no need for fear.

Through thick and thin, we chart our course,
Navigating storms with luck and grace.
In every step, love is the force,
A map of joy in every place.

The stars attend our evening talks,
Lighting paths with their silver beams.
In the quiet, the world unlocks,
Together, we chase our wild dreams.

From mountain peaks to ocean tides,
Adventure whispers, come explore.
With love as our eternal guide,
Together, we're forever more.

In the journey that holds no end,
Each moment a treasure to find.
Side by side, together we mend,
With love's compass forever blind.

Navigating Affection's Waters

In a boat made of dreams we sail,
Across a sea of endless hope.
With love as wind, we shall not fail,
Together, we learn how to cope.

The horizon calls with hues so bright,
Painted skies mirror our hearts' glow.
In the stars, we find our light,
Guiding us where warm breezes flow.

As gentle waves lap at the shore,
Sweet moments drift in timeless air.
In silence, we seek to explore,
With every glance, a love affair.

Through whirlpools that challenge our path,
We stand together, strong and true.
With laughter, we weather the wrath,
In affection's waters, me and you.

So let the tides honor our love,
As we sail through each passing day.
With hearts like the sky up above,
We'll navigate life, come what may.

The Measure of Affection

In whispers soft, our hearts align,
With every glance, a bond divine.
Moments shared, a gentle grace,
Your laughter lights my quiet space.

Each tender touch, a promise sealed,
In silent vows, our truth revealed.
Through trials faced, we stand as one,
In love's embrace, we have begun.

Time may pass, but we will stay,
Guided by love, come what may.
A measure of affection pure,
In every heartbeat, we endure.

Through stormy seas, we find the way,
With warmth that never fades away.
Together, strong, we weather all,
In your sweet arms, I will not fall.

So let us dance beneath the stars,
With hope alight, despite the scars.
In every moment, love's refrain,
Our measure deep, in joy and pain.

Tethered Dreams

In twilight's glow, our visions weave,
A tapestry of dreams that believe.
With every thought, we chase the night,
Tethered whispers, hearts take flight.

Through foggy paths, hand in hand,
We share our hopes, a promised land.
In silent vows, we're ever bound,
With every heartbeat, love is found.

Stars above, like dreams unfold,
A story written, brave and bold.
In every wish, a piece of us,
With faith unwavering, in love we trust.

In restless seas, we find our North,
A gentle pull, bringing us forth.
Together we rise, in joy and fear,
Each moment cherished, dreamers near.

With eyes that see what's yet to come,
In tender graces, we are one.
With tethered threads, our hearts entwine,
In dreams we dwell, forever shine.

The Underlying Rhythm

In heartbeats soft, a pulse we share,
A rhythm coursing through the air.
Like music played on strings of fate,
In every sigh, we resonate.

With whispered tunes, we dance along,
A melody where we belong.
In perfect time, our souls do sway,
In harmony, we find our way.

Through fleeting days and endless nights,
We follow pulses, spark ignites.
In every glance, a song revealed,
In love's refrain, our truth concealed.

With every step, the tempo grows,
In gentle waves, affection flows.
The underlying rhythm calls,
In life's grand dance, true love enthralls.

In tender beats, our stories blend,
As we embrace, the world can bend.
In fate's embrace, we find our sound,
The underlying rhythm, love profound.

Merging Paths

In twilight's glow, our paths converge,
A journey forged, where dreams emerge.
With each soft step, our spirits weave,
In harmony, we learn to believe.

Through forest trails and rivers wide,
With open hearts, we walk side by side.
In shared adventures, laughter flows,
In silent moments, connection grows.

In morning light, the world awakes,
In every choice, a love that stakes.
With courage bold, we face the way,
In each embrace, our fears allay.

With every turn, new sights unfold,
In stories shared, our hearts are bold.
The merging paths, a dance of fate,
In tangled roots, we resonate.

Hand in hand, we venture forth,
With dreams that guide us, endless worth.
In every heartbeat, journeys blend,
Together strong, until the end.

The Sway of Souls

In the quiet whispers of the night,
Two souls dance under pale moonlight.
A rhythm gentle, soft, and slow,
Bound together in an ageless flow.

Through the shadows of the past,
Their connection shines, built to last.
Echoes of laughter, sweet and clear,
A melody known, they both hold dear.

With every heartbeat, every sigh,
They weave a tapestry, you and I.
In the spaces where silence thrives,
The sway of souls forever survives.

Among the stars, hand in hand,
They navigate this vast expanse,
Hearts entwined, they take their stand,
In the universe's sacred dance.

Through trials faced and battles won,
Their light shines bright, a rising sun.
In the journey, together they find,
The beauty born from heart and mind.

Holding Hands

Fingers entwined in a tender hold,
Stories of warmth in silence told.
Every heartbeat, a promise made,
In the light of love, never to fade.

Through the storms and the gentle rain,
Holding hands, they share the pain.
Strength in unity, never apart,
Two souls linked, one beating heart.

In the quiet moments, smiles exchanged,
A world created, beautifully arranged.
Pathways carved by journeys shared,
In each other's gaze, they are prepared.

Through laughter's echo, through sorrow's sigh,
Each grasp a testament, they can't deny.
Together facing what life demands,
With courage found in holding hands.

Time may shift, but love will stay,
In every dawn, in every day.
Through thick and thin and all that's grand,
Forever strong, still holding hands.

Holding Hope

In the shadows where dreams might fade,
Hope stands tall, unafraid.
A flicker bright within the dark,
Guiding hearts, igniting a spark.

With every breath, whisper a dream,
Fostering strength in gentle gleam.
Through trials faced and doubts that creep,
Holding hope, the promise to keep.

Moments of doubt and fear may rise,
Yet in the deep, hope never lies.
Through stormy paths and winding roads,
It bears the weight, it shares the loads.

In the warmth of dawn, rebirth begins,
Hope dances lightly, through losses and wins.
A beacon bright when the night is long,
Ever resilient, ever strong.

So hold it close, this fragile thread,
In every word that's left unsaid.
For in its embrace, we find our way,
Holding hope, day by day.

Between the Tension

In the spaces where silence reigns,
Whispers of truth, suspending chains.
Hearts entwined, yet worlds apart,
Between the tension, a restless heart.

Unspoken words hang in the air,
Fragile feelings, unaware.
Two souls reaching, stretching wide,
Navigating waves of ebb and tide.

Yet in the clash where shadows play,
Lies the spark to find the way.
In every struggle, wisdom grows,
Between the tension, a garden sows.

Through the conflict and the pain,
Comes the chance to rise again.
In understanding, lessons learned,
Between the tension, hope can turn.

So breathe in deep, let go of fears,
Embrace the moments, shed the tears.
For love can flourish in the space,
Between the tension, find your place.

Bridges of Understanding

Two different worlds, yet close they stand,
Building bridges with soft, skilled hands.
Through laughter shared and stories told,
A connection forged, a bond of gold.

In every glance, a path revealed,
Hearts opening wide, no longer sealed.
With each step taken, layers unwind,
Bridges of understanding, hearts aligned.

Through diverse colors, cultures collide,
In unity's embrace, they take pride.
With open minds, they navigate,
The beauty found in the love they create.

In shared experiences, wisdom flows,
Watering seeds of friendship that grows.
With patience and trust, they each explore,
Bridges of understanding, forevermore.

So let us listen, let us learn,
In every heart, a fire to burn.
For in these bridges, we can find,
A world of hope, intertwined.

Crafted Connections

In threads of gold and silver spun,
We weave our stories, one by one.
Through laughter, tears, and silent sighs,
Connections bloom beneath the skies.

Each heartbeat echoes in the night,
A tapestry of love and light.
With every glance, a bond takes shape,
In this vast world, we find escape.

Seasons change, yet still we stand,
Together strong, we join our hands.
In woven paths, our souls entwine,
Crafted connections, purely divine.

In storms and sun, we find our way,
Guided by trust, come what may.
With every choice, a thread we drop,
Building bridges that never stop.

We nurture roots and watch them grow,
In the garden of life, we sow.
Treasured moments, simple and sweet,
In crafted connections, we are complete.

The Dance of Dependence

A gentle sway, a heartfelt tune,
We find our grace beneath the moon.
In every step, a trust we share,
A dance of hearts in open air.

With every pause, a breath we take,
The fragile lines of give and take.
In shadows deep, we learn to shine,
Together bound, your hand in mine.

Rhythms shift, yet never fade,
We spin in circles, unafraid.
In the balance, we find our stride,
The dance of dependence, side by side.

Through highs and lows, we move as one,
In each embrace, the battles won.
With whispered words, we paint our past,
In this dance, sweet love will last.

As time flows on, our steps grow bold,
Together warm against the cold.
In every heartbeat, every glance,
We celebrate this sacred dance.

Interwoven Lives

In the loom of life, we intertwine,
Lives interwoven, yours and mine.
Each unique thread, a story told,
In vibrant colors, rich and bold.

Through trials faced and joy embraced,
In every moment, hearts are graced.
The fabric strong, yet finely spun,
In interwoven lives, we are one.

Every whisper, every sigh,
A tapestry of you and I.
In the patterns, we find our song,
Together bound, where we belong.

The weaving grows with every year,
In laughter shared and hidden fear.
We patch the frays and mend the seams,
In this grand quilt, we build our dreams.

As seasons change and time moves on,
In every thread, our love lives strong.
Interwoven lives, a dance so rare,
In unity, we find our care.

Weaving Between Worlds

In twilight's glow, we find our place,
Weaving between worlds, a sacred space.
With threads of hope and dreams in tow,
Our journey starts with every glow.

Through veils of time, we glance and see,
The beauty held in you and me.
Each step we take, a bridge to span,
In this great dance, we learn to plan.

With whispers soft, our spirits soar,
Together brave, we seek for more.
In the tapestry of night and day,
We find our voices, come what may.

The worlds collide, but we remain,
In every joy and every pain.
The threads weave tight and gentle, bold,
In between worlds, our love unfolds.

As stars align, our paths are clear,
In harmony, we shed our fear.
We weave the tales of lives well-known,
Creating magic, a world our own.

Heartstrings in Harmony

In twilight's glow, we softly sway,
The world fades, as we drift away.
Notes of love in the evening air,
A melody that's sweet and rare.

With every glance, our souls ignite,
Two hearts entwined, a wondrous sight.
Together we dance, hand in hand,
In a rhythm only we understand.

Through whispered words and quiet grace,
Our laughter echoes in this place.
Like rivers merging, we unite,
In harmony, we find our light.

The music swells, the stars align,
In every beat, your heart is mine.
With every measure, love does grow,
In perfect time, the world below.

So let us stay, in this embrace,
Where every heart can find its space.
In twilight's glow, we softly sway,
Forever bound, we'll find our way.

Ties of Understanding

Beneath the surface, silence speaks,
In knowing glances, love seeks.
Not every thought needs to be said,
For in the quiet, hearts are read.

We share the burdens, trade the fears,
With whispered hopes and dried-up tears.
A tapestry of dreams we weave,
In the fabric of trust, we believe.

From distant worlds, our paths aligned,
In every moment, we're entwined.
Understanding flows like a stream,
In the light of day and night's dream.

So let us cherish this sweet bond,
In every silence, we respond.
With subtle cues that we both know,
In ties of understanding, we glow.

Together we rise, together we fall,
In every tear, we hear the call.
With hearts wide open, we shall stand,
In this dance of life, hand in hand.

Holding the Line

In the tempest's roar, we find our place,
Side by side, we face the chase.
With sturdy hearts, we weather the storm,
In the chaos, love keeps us warm.

Through trials faced and shadows cast,
We hold on tight, our ties will last.
In every struggle, we find our grace,
Together we move, a steady pace.

When darkness looms and hope seems dim,
I'll be your light, I'll never swim.
In the waves of doubt, we'll stay aligned,
With every heartbeat, hearts combined.

So here we stand, through thick and thin,
In the depths of loss, we both will win.
With every challenge, our spirits shine,
Bound by strength, holding the line.

In unity's grasp, we will abide,
With arms entwined, we turn the tide.
Together we'll rise, through all that's given,
In this love, forever driven.

The Gentle Tug

In the softest moments, a pull we feel,
A gentle tug, love's quiet seal.
With every heartbeat, the ties connect,
In tender whispers, we reflect.

The world around may fade away,
But in your light, I choose to stay.
With every smile, the pull grows strong,
In your embrace, I know I belong.

A quiet force, unseen, yet bold,
In every touch, a story told.
Through distant shores and paths unknown,
The gentle tug leads me back home.

With every tear, a lesson learned,
In love's embrace, we are returned.
No need for words, our hearts comply,
In the gentle tug, we learn to fly.

So let us cherish this bond so deep,
In every promise, our hearts we keep.
With gentle tugs, we find our way,
In love's pure light, we brightly stay.

Harmonizing Differences

In the tapestry of life, we weave,
Threads of colors that softly cleave,
Marking paths both new and old,
In unity, our stories unfold.

Voices merge like rivers flow,
Echoes of laughter, soft and slow,
Each note distinct, yet in refrain,
Together we dance through joy and pain.

A symphony of hearts at play,
Celebrating night and day,
What divides us, we transform,
In harmony, we find our warm.

With open arms, we share the day,
Bridging gaps in our own way,
Learning to cherish every tone,
In differences, we find our home.

So let us sing, let us create,
A world where love can elevate,
In this blend, our spirits rise,
Harmonizing beneath the skies.

The Weight of Affection

Beneath the stars, where silence reigns,
The weight of love, like gentle chains,
Holding close what words can't say,
In each heartbeat, we find our way.

Soft whispers spill in the night air,
Promises made beyond compare,
Each gesture carries the depth of truth,
Embracing the essence of our youth.

In the warmth of an embrace, we see,
Reflections of who we aim to be,
The burden sweet, like honeyed gold,
In every glance, our tales are told.

Through trials faced, we stand as one,
In storms that clash and shadows spun,
Together we rise, with strength anew,
In love's embrace, our spirits grew.

So let us cherish this sacred weight,
In every moment, we create,
A legacy forged in time's own hand,
Bound by affection, forever we stand.

In the Balance of Being

In the dance of dusk and dawn,
Life's delicate threads are drawn,
Each step a choice, a path we tread,
In every moment, we feel and read.

Echoes of laughter, whispers of tears,
The balance sways through all our years,
Courage found in fragile grace,
In stillness, we find our place.

With shadows casting doubts at night,
Hope flickers softly, a guiding light,
In chaos, we seek the serene,
Finding joy in what might have been.

In unity, our strength aligns,
Through challenges, our spirit shines,
Together we dance, a timeless song,
In the balance, we all belong.

Let each heartbeat anchor our flight,
In this journey of wrongs and rights,
For in the balance, love shall stay,
Guiding us through each passing day.

The Junction of Hearts

At the corner where dreams collide,
Two paths converge, with hope as guide,
In curious glances, a spark ignites,
A union forged in starry nights.

Every heartbeat writes a tale,
A reverie where love prevails,
In whispers shared and stories spun,
The junction shines in the morning sun.

With every step, we redefine,
The spaces where our souls entwine,
Hand in hand, we pave the way,
In this meeting, we find our sway.

Through laughter's echoes and silence deep,
In the bonds we've sworn to keep,
Together we navigate the maze,
At the turn where affection stays.

So let us cherish this sacred place,
In our journey, a warm embrace,
For at the junction of our hearts,
A beautiful symphony starts.